Old Te

Treasures

Reflections and prayers
on favourite Bible passages

Nick Fawcett

kevin
mayhew

First published in 2004 by

KEVIN MAYHEW LTD
Buxhall, Stowmarket, Suffolk, IP14 3BW
E-mail: info@kevinmayhewltd.com

KINGSGATE PUBLISHING INC
1000 Pannell Street, Suite G, Columbia, MO 65201
E-mail: sales@kingsgatepublishing.com

The material in this book first appeared in *Daily Prayer*
and *The Fawcett Bible Studies*.

9 8 7 6 5 4 3 2 1 0

ISBN 1 84417 262 7
Catalogue No. 1500704

Cover design by Angela Selfe
Edited by Katherine Laidler
Typesetting by Fiona Connell-Finch

Printed and bound in Great Britain

Contents

Introduction

Some passages of the Bible stand out in the memory, don't they? While the whole of Scripture is important, neglected at our peril, certain verses capture our imagination or speak to us in a way that few others can begin to. Who can forget the words of the 23rd Psalm, the parables of Jesus, or the wonderful teaching of Paul in 1 Corinthians 13 on the gift of love? These are just some of the countless passages to have encouraged, comforted, strengthened and inspired Christians across the centuries.

We must, of course, beware of being too selective when it comes to reading the Bible, or we will end up avoiding whatever might challenge our particular viewpoint, thus effectively closing our ears to anything that God might wish to say to us. He has an uncanny knack of speaking through the most unlikely of verses, stretching our horizons and disturbing the comfortable status quo. On the other hand, well-loved verses can remind us of the underlying realities of the gospel, offering reassurance in times of doubt, support in times of challenge and hope in times of despair. Some, indeed, become so familiar to us that they seem almost like old friends. We may even know them off by heart, yet their power to challenge, inspire and encourage remains undiminished, God continuing to speak through them in new and wonderful ways.

In this short compilation I have drawn upon my book *Daily Prayer* and various volumes of my Bible Study series to offer brief reflections on 16 unforgettable passages from the Old Testament, each supplemented by a simple closing prayer. The selection is inevitably a personal one, but I suspect many of the passages I have chosen will also feature among your own personal favourites. It is my hope that they will speak as powerfully to you as they have to me.

NICK FAWCETT

Genesis 28:10-13a, 16-17

An unexpected encounter

Jacob left Beersheba and set off towards Haran, but, since the sun was setting, he stopped off at a convenient spot en route. Taking a stone he found there, he tucked it under his head and lay down. And in his dreams he saw a ladder rising up from the ground, its top reaching into heaven, the angels of God climbing up and down it. And the Lord appeared, standing beside him, and said, 'I am the Lord, the God of your father Abraham and the God of Isaac . . .' Jacob woke and, suddenly afraid, exclaimed, 'Surely the Lord is in this place, and I wasn't aware of it! What an awe-inspiring place this is! It is nothing less than the house of God, the very gate of heaven.'

Reflection

Of all the great figures of the Old Testament, few showed less initial promise than Jacob. He comes across as an opportunist and a cheat, callously tricking his brother Esau out of his birthright, and then compounding this with the shameful deception of his father. As he made his way towards Haran, it was, no doubt, with a smug sense of self-satisfaction at having secured the prospect of a highly prosperous future. The last thing on his mind would have been God.

God, though, had other ideas, confronting him during the night in a vivid and unforgettable dream. It was the beginning of a gradual change in Jacob's life. No, he didn't change overnight – far from it. He continued in many ways to be the wily schemer of old. Yet the seeds had been sown; God had met with him and opened up a new perspective on life and the beginning of a living and personal relationship. It was one, ultimately, that would see Jacob revered as one of the founding fathers of the Jewish faith and a celebrated 'man of God'.

Here, in miniature, is the message of the gospel: the truth that God, in his love, seeks us out and calls us, not through any merit on our part but by his grace alone, accepting us despite our faults and reshaping our lives through his transforming power. Never, then, give up on yourself, nor give up on others, for God is able to change lives beyond all expectations.

Prayer

Living God,
   I thank you that before ever I thought of seeking you,
   you sought me;
   that you had time for me
   even when I lived only for myself.
Teach me that you are always at work,
   in my life and in the world,
   confronting, calling, renewing and redeeming,
   taking the most unpromising of situations
   and unlikely of people
   and transforming them through your power.
Open my eyes, then, to your searching presence
   and sovereign grace,
   through Jesus Christ my Lord.
Amen.

Deuteronomy 33:27

The everlasting arms of God

The eternal God is your never-ending home, and supporting you always are his everlasting arms.

Reflection

Anyone who has had children will never forget the magical moment when they first began to walk. It was probably a few stumbling steps, no more, but it marked another stage in the journey of life. For such steps to happen, however, one thing is usually needed – a doting parent close at hand with arms outstretched, waiting to catch their offspring should they start to totter and fall. The knowledge that someone is there to offer support is all important, giving children the confidence they need to take not just their first faltering steps en route to walking but also their first steps in so much else – exploring new horizons, meeting new people, starting a new school, taking on new responsibilities and so on. Sometimes this will prove easy; at other times difficult; but always there will be – or at least should be – the knowledge that a loved one is there for them, ready to pick them up, offer a comforting embrace, and urge them onwards.

So it is with God. He constantly watches over us, ready to offer a helping hand in times of need, to lift us up when we stumble, to comfort us in sorrow and reassure us in times of fear. Even in death, those arms are there, enfolding us as we meet the last enemy and leading us to life eternal. God delights in *us* as much as *we* do in our own children. Whatever the future holds, then, we can rest secure, safe in his everlasting arms.

Prayer

Living God,
    embrace me in your arms,
    encircle me with your grace
    and enfold me in your love,
    for Jesus' sake.
Amen.

Joshua 1:1-6
I will be with you

Following the death of the Lord's servant Moses, the Lord spoke to Joshua son of Nun, Moses' assistant, saying, 'My servant Moses is dead. Now advance with all the people of Israel and cross the Jordan into the land that I am giving them. I will readily give to you everywhere that you set foot, as I promised to Moses. From the wilderness and the Lebanon as far as the great river, the river Euphrates, all the land of the Hittites and on towards the Great Sea in the west shall be your territory. Nobody will be able to withstand you all the days of your life. Just as I was with Moses, so I will be with you; I will not fail or forsake you. Be strong and of good courage, for you will lead this people to take possession of the land that I swore to their ancestors to give them.'

Reflection

'Come with me.' How often have we asked that of somebody? Whether it's of parents as we start a new school, a partner as we go into hospital for a consultation, or a friend as we go to a party, we value having somebody to share things with, to offer moral support, a word of encouragement, a shoulder to lean on or a helping hand. As the old saying put it, 'A problem shared is a problem halved.' Sadly, such support is not always there when we need it, but, as the experience of Joshua reminds us, we are never wholly alone, for God has promised always to be with us. How much that meant to Joshua cannot be overemphasised, as, after long years of wandering in the wilderness, he found himself entrusted with the responsibility of taking over from Moses and leading the Israelites into the Promised Land. Alone, he would have buckled, unable to meet the challenge, but he knew God was with him wherever he went.

So it is for us today. We may not always be conscious of God's presence – indeed, at times we may still feel very much alone – but he is by our side nonetheless, his love enfolding us, his grace renewing, his power supporting and his hand guiding. When we stumble, he will be there to pick us up; when we grow weary, he will renew our strength; when we are unsure of the way ahead, he will be there to guide. Wherever we are, whatever we face, he will give us strength to continue, for he does not simply call us to a journey; he also travels with us!

Prayer

Living God,
    give me the faith and commitment I need
    to walk your way,
    trusting in your guidance,
    responding to your call,
    confident that, whatever difficulties and disappointments
    I may face,
    you will equip me to meet them.
Amen.

Ruth 1:8-17

Voice of the outsider

Naomi instructed her daughters-in-law, 'You must both return to your mother's house. May the Lord be gracious to you, as you have been to the deceased and to me, and may he help each of you to find refuge in the house of your husband.' She kissed them, but they sobbed loudly, and replied, 'No, we want to go back with you to your people.' 'Turn back, my daughters,' insisted Naomi; 'why do you want to go with me? Is there any prospect of me bearing other sons whom you might marry one day? Turn back, my daughters, make your own way, for I'm well past having a husband. Let's face it, even if there was a chance of me getting married tonight and bearing sons, would you honestly want to wait for them to grow up? Would you avoid marrying in the meantime? No, my daughters, whatever bitterness you have faced has been all the worse for me, because the Lord's hand has turned against me.' Once more the tears flowed. Orpah kissed her mother-in-law and set off, but Ruth held on to Naomi. 'Look,' Naomi told her, 'your sister-in-law has returned to her people and her gods; go after her.' But Ruth answered, 'Do not urge me to turn back and abandon you. Wherever you go, I will go; wherever you stop, I will stop; your people will be my people, and your God my God. Where you die, I will die and be buried. In God's name, I swear that not even death will part me from you!'

Reflection

The book of Ruth was written with the intention to shock. It may not do so now, but there's little doubt it would have raised hackles and stirred controversy among its first readers. Taking centre stage is a woman in a male-dominated world, a woman moreover who is half-Moabite rather than a pure Jew! The idea that God might work through her, offering an example to follow and a lesson in faith would, to many in Israel, have seemed simply laughable. Yet that, of course, is the way things turn out, Ruth's faith, courage and commitment nowhere better exemplified than in that wonderful protestation of loyalty: 'Wherever you go, I will go; wherever you stop, I will stop; your people will be my people, and your God my God. Where you die, I will die and be buried' (Ruth 1:16-17).

On one level, Ruth's story is one of devotion beyond the call of duty, challenging us to consider the depth of commitment we show to one another, but, on a deeper level, it speaks also of God: the way each of us has a place in his heart and a part to play in his purpose, irrespective of creed, colour or culture; the way he is able to work through those we might least expect; and the way his love extends beyond the artificial barriers that keep us apart. In a world as divided as it has ever been – scarred by suspicions concerning terrorism, asylum seekers, immigration and so much else – we urgently need to hear that message. Are we open to those around us, ready to listen and learn from those we might consider outsiders? Are we ready to be stretched, to have our comfortable preconceptions undermined and our prejudices chal-lenged? Are we ready to consider new ideas, different points of view and fresh insights? God may be speaking today in unexpected ways and places. Are we ready to listen?

Prayer

Loving God,
    open our hearts to one another,
    to others,
    and, above all, to you,
    so that we might love you truly,
    serve you faithfully,
    and recognise your voice,
    wherever,
    whenever,
    and through whomsoever
    you choose to speak.
Amen.

1 Samuel 17:43-45, 48-49

David and Goliath

Goliath said to David, 'Am I a dog, that you approach me with sticks?' And he swore at David using the name of his gods. 'Come on,' he taunted, 'attack me, and I will give your flesh to the birds of the air and to the beasts of the field.' But David responded, 'You confront me with sword, spear and javelin, but I confront you in the name of the Lord of hosts, the God of the armies of Israel, whom you have defied.' When the Philistine advanced towards him, David darted forward to do battle with him. Reaching down into his bag, he took out a stone, slung it, and struck the Philistine on the forehead; the stone sank into his forehead, and he collapsed face downwards on the ground.

Reflection

It's always pleasing, isn't it, when a midget turns the tables on a giant. Whether it be a non-league football team defeating its premier league relations, a village store fighting off competition from an out-of-town supermarket, or a local pressure group resisting the plans of a multinational company, our hearts warm to tales of the underdog come good.

Little wonder, then, that the tale of David and Goliath has stood the test of time, told and retold by countless generations across the years. Their celebrated encounter is a classic example of the underdog coming out on top, triumphing against all the odds. Few plots have been more extensively used by writers over the centuries, but what makes this story so special is that it is rooted in fact, not fiction. It offers an enduring testimony to the way God is able to help each one of us measure up to the obstacles we face and, no matter how great they may be, to emerge victorious over them.

Prayer

Sovereign God,
    instead of seeing what *I can't* do,
    teach me to see what *you can,*
      through Jesus Christ, my Lord and Saviour.
Amen.

1 Kings 19:11b-13
The still, small voice

The Lord was passing by, and a gust of wind arose, so strong that it shook the mountain and shattered rocks before him, but the Lord was not in the wind. After that came an earthquake, but the Lord was not in the earthquake, and after the earthquake came fire, but the Lord was not in the fire; and after the fire there was simply the sound of silence. When Elijah heard this, he hid his face in his cloak, went out and stood at the entrance of the cave. Then a voice came to him, asking, 'Why are you here, Elijah?'

Reflection

The story of Elijah's encounter with God on the slopes of Mount Horeb has inspired countless sermons and innumerable prayers, not to mention the celebrated hymn, 'Dear Lord and Father of mankind, forgive our foolish ways'. What, though, is it all about, and what, in particular, is the significance of the 'sound of silence', or the 'still small voice', as other translations put it?

There are probably several equally valid answers to those questions, but one that occurred to me rereading these verses is that this incident may perhaps have something to say concerning those times when God seems far away. Elijah looks for God in the mighty wind, surely a sign of his power, but no, he is not there. He looks again in the mighty earthquake, but again, no. Then there is the fire, reminiscent of the cloudy pillar that guided the people of Israel, and you can almost imagine Elijah thinking, 'This must be him!' – but yet again it isn't. Yet, just when the prophet may have been giving up hope, there comes that voice like a gentle whisper – so unpretentious, so insignificant, you could almost miss it. Was this God's way of telling Elijah he is present in the ordinary and banal moments of life even when it doesn't look like it? I may simply be clutching at straws here, but I like to think this interpretation contains a grain of truth, for, let's face it, occasions when God is dramatically at work are all too rare. The fact is that he is equally present in the humdrum business of daily life, even when we struggle to catch sight of him; perhaps there most of all.

Prayer

Gracious God,
    help me to hear again your still small voice,
    your word even in the silence,
    and so may I recognise that,
    however little I may realise it,
    you are always there and always active,
    through Jesus Christ my Lord.
Amen.

Psalm 23
The Lord's my shepherd

The Lord is my shepherd, I want for nothing. He makes me lie down in fertile pastures; he leads me beside tranquil waters; he restores my soul. He leads me in right paths for his name's sake. Even though I walk through the darkest of valleys, I fear no evil; for you are with me, O God, your rod and staff a constant source of comfort. You prepare a table before me in the presence of my foes; you anoint my head with oil; my cup brims over. Surely goodness and mercy will accompany me all my days, and I shall dwell in the house of the Lord my whole life long.

Reflection

Few passages of Scripture have brought greater comfort and inspiration across the centuries than the 23rd Psalm. Even those with little or no interest in Christianity tend to find it meaningful, if only from hearing it read or sung at the funeral of a friend or loved one, the words resonating at some deep unconscious level. Perhaps one of the secrets of its enduring popularity is that David himself, in his youth, was a shepherd. In other words, when he wrote 'The Lord is my shepherd' he knew what he was talking about, the words rich with personal associations. Here was no sentimental comparison. It was rather the testimony of someone who understood the commitment and devotion that shepherding requires and who, in an outpouring of wonder, realised that here was an illustration of God's astonishing love for all his people.

For us, that love has been revealed all the more wonderfully through Jesus Christ and his willingness to offer his life for our sakes. He is the one who walked through that darkest of valleys, the valley of the shadow of death, so that truly we need fear no evil. Nothing now, in earth or heaven can ever finally separate us from the love of God expressed through him.

Prayer

Living God,

    lead me on through the changes and chances of this life,

    and through the valley of the shadow of death,

    until I am safely gathered into your kingdom

    and my journey is done.

In the meantime,

    help me to stay as close to you

    as you stay close to me,

    through Jesus Christ my Lord.

Amen.

Psalm 139:7-12

A God here, there and everywhere

Where can I evade your spirit? Where can I flee from your presence? If I soar up to heaven, you are there; if I make my bed in Sheol, you are there. If I sail on the wings of the morning and settle at the uttermost limits of the sea, even there your hand will lead me, your right hand holding me firm. If I say, 'Surely darkness will steal over me, night will envelop me', darkness is not dark to you; the night is as bright as day; for you both dark and light are the same.

Reflection

We seek him here, we seek him there, those Frenchies seek him everywhere. Is he in heaven? – Is he in hell? That demmed elusive Pimpernel? So run the famous lines of Baroness Orczy concerning the renowned character of her novels: the Scarlet Pimpernel. Come what may, the dashing hero invariably turns up at the right time and place; no one and nowhere, it seems, beyond his reach. Such, of course, is the prerogative of fictional heroes.

With God, though, it is no fiction. He is the one before and beyond all, yet the one who is with us, here and now; the ruler over space and time, yet the one constantly by our side. No one is outside his love, nowhere beyond his grace, no situation outside his concern – not even death itself can separate us from his sovereign purpose in Christ. Whether you see him or whether you don't, whether you sense he is close or feel he is far away, remember this: he is here, there and everywhere.

Prayer

Living God,
  I thank you that you are not just with me here in prayer
  but with me always in the daily round of life;
  as much there as anywhere,
  waiting to meet, lead and bless me.
Help me to glimpse your presence
  and to live each moment
  conscious that you are by my side,
  to your praise and glory.
Amen.

Ecclesiastes 3:1-8
A time for everything

There is a season for everything, and a time for every activity under heaven: a time to be born and a time to die; a time to plant and a time to uproot; a time to kill and a time to heal; a time to pull down and a time to build up; a time to cry and a time to laugh; a time to grieve and a time to dance; a time to scatter stones and a time to gather them; a time to embrace and a time not to embrace; a time to seek and a time to lose; a time to keep and a time to throw away; a time to tear and a time to mend; a time for silence and a time for speech; a time to love and a time to hate; a time for war and a time for peace.

Reflection

Time's a funny thing, isn't it? One moment we can feel down in the dumps and the next on top of the world; today life can seem full of trouble but tomorrow it may appear full of promise. Our experience is always changing and life is constantly moving on. In some ways that is a sobering prospect, reminding us all too starkly of our mortality, yet where would we be without the variety that the passing of time brings – the passing of the seasons, the birth and growth of a child, the anticipation of a special event and, of course, our hope in Christ?

The secret with time is to know how to respond to it; understanding what mood or action is appropriate for a particular occasion. Should we put the past behind us or hold on to it? Should we grasp the nettle or admit defeat? Should we stand up for our principles or be ready to bend? We face a host of questions like these every day, and no answer is uniformly correct. We need constantly to seek God's guidance, for he is the one who holds time itself in his hands, the one who in all the changes and chances of this life will not change.

Prayer

God of past, present and future,
the same yesterday, today and tomorrow,
teach me to use each moment wisely,
always open to your guidance,
always awake to your will.
Teach me to see time not as a threat but as your gift,
and so may I live life to the full,
as you desire.
Amen.

Isaiah 6:1-8

Send me

In the year King Uzziah died, I saw the Lord enthroned on high, exalted over all; and the hem of his robe filled the temple. Seraphim waited upon him, each having six wings; two of which they used to cover their faces, two to cover their feet, and two to fly. They called back and forth to one another, saying, 'Holy, holy, holy is the Lord of hosts; the whole earth is full of his glory.' At the sound of their voices the threshold shook and the house was filled with smoke. And I cried out, 'Woe am I! I am lost, for I am a man of unclean lips, living among a people of unclean lips; yet with my own eyes I have seen the King, the Lord of hosts!' Then one of the seraphim flew to me, holding in his hand a burning coal taken from the altar with a pair of tongs. The seraph touched my mouth with it and said, 'Since this has touched your lips, your guilt is no more and your sin is done away with.' Then I heard the voice of the Lord saying, 'Whom shall I send? Who will go for me?' And I said, 'Here I am; send me!'

Reflection

One of the tragedies of the Church is that it has acquired a reputation for being smug, self-righteous, holier than thou. How this has happened I do not know, for while some in the Church are more than ready to sit in judgement, by far the majority are too aware of their own faults to point the accusing finger at others. Such, at least, has been my experience. The heart of the Christian message is one of forgiveness rather than judgement; about the God who is ready to accept us as we are rather than as we should be. Of course this involves a desire to change, but it begins and ends with God rather than us. The truth of that is most clearly demonstrated through Christ, but it was discovered centuries before by countless others.

So it was that a young man, worshipping in the temple of Jerusalem, suddenly found himself faced by the call of God. Hopelessly inadequate though he felt, burdened by a profound sense of unworthiness, Isaiah discovered that God is always ready to take the initiative in offering us a fresh start. All that he needed to do was respond, and with that began one of the most remarkable prophetic ministries of all time, his words touching the hearts of generations across the centuries. All *we* need to do is respond in turn, to discover the new beginning God longs to bring us, a new beginning not of our own making but entirely of his grace.

Prayer

Gracious God,
    renew me through your Spirit,
    redeem me through the grace of Christ
    and remake me through your great love,
    so that I might receive each moment as a fresh start
    and consecrate it to your service.
Amen.

Isaiah 55:6-9
The God beyond us

Seek out the Lord while you can still find him; cry out to him while he seems close. Let evildoers turn from their foolish ways, and sinners abandon their unworthy thoughts. Let them come back to the Lord our God, so that he may forgive them, for his nature is unreservedly to pardon. For your thoughts are nothing like mine, says the Lord, nor do your ways even begin to resemble my own. As the heavens are far above the earth, so my ways and thoughts are infinitely above anything you can ever begin to do or think.

Reflection

Few passages of Scripture mean more to me than Isaiah 55:8-9. Why? Because these verses speak to the many and varied situations of life as few others even begin to, reminding us of the sheer 'otherness' of God, yet, at the same time, of his incredible grace. When times are hard to understand, faith seeming to fly in the face of reason, here is a reminder that behind the riddle of our fleeting existence lies a deeper purpose making sense of it all. When life is good, brimming over with promise, here is a testimony to the God who is able to bless us still further in ways untold and unimagined. When we're troubled by feelings of guilt and failure, convinced that no one in their right minds can possibly have time for us, we find here the assurance that God is always ready to forgive and forget, his grace defying human logic. So I could go on. Isaiah's testimony reminds us of a God whose greatness is beyond words, whose awesomeness defies expression, who is more powerful, caring, gracious and good than the human mind can ever comprehend. It calls us to a humble acknowledgement of our flawed knowledge of the divine, yet speaks simultaneously of the wonderful adventure of faith to which all are called; an adventure which never ends.

Prayer

Sovereign God,
    all too often I have lost sight of your greatness,
    settling instead for a picture of you
    I feel comfortable with.
I have frustrated your will
    through the smallness of my vision.
I have missed opportunities to serve you
    through the narrowness of my horizons.
I have denied myself your mercy
    through the confines I place upon your grace.
Repeatedly I have presumed that your ways are *my* ways
    and your thoughts *my* thoughts,
    forgetting that you are beyond words
    or human understanding.
Forgive me,
    and teach me never to underestimate
    the awesomeness of your being
    or the extent of your love.
Amen.

Isaiah 55:10-11

A God we can depend on

As rain and snow fall from on high and do not return until they have irrigated the earth causing it to germinate and blossom, and yielding seed for future sowing and bread for nourishment – so it is likewise with the word I speak; it will never prove fruitless, but will accomplish my purpose, invariably achieving that which I sent it out to do.

Reflection

I'd posted my letter and was waiting eagerly for a reply, each day growing increasingly impatient at the delay. 'What could be keeping them?' I wondered. How much longer would it be? Three weeks later the letter arrived – not the letter I was anticipating but the one I had sent, with a curt message scribbled across the front: 'Return to sender. Address not known.' Life can be like that sometimes, can't it? We think we've done something, only to find it's gone wrong. We believe we've completed a job only to discover it needs doing all over again.

With God, it's different. What he says he will do, he does. What he accomplishes is achieved once and for all. The point in Isaiah is driven home: 'My will shall prevail, and I will fulfil my purpose . . . I have spoken, and I will make it happen; I have planned, and I will accomplish it' (46:11). If Isaiah understood that truth, then we surely should recognise it all the more, for it has been proven most graphically and wonderfully in Christ, God's Word living and breathing among us, sharing our humanity, walking our earth – the ultimate fulfilment of God's promise. His living, dying and rising among us is the ultimate demonstration of God's faithfulness, our assurance that we can trust him like no other, certain he will not fail us. Hold on to his promises, trust in his word, have faith in the future, for whatever else may fail, he will not.

Prayer

Living God,
    I praise you for the assurance
    that your will shall be done
    and your purpose shall finally triumph.
I thank you that in all the changing circumstances of life
    you are constantly active,
    day by day working to fulfil your sovereign purpose.
Teach me, then, to live each moment with total confidence,
    knowing that, though all else may fail, you will not.
Teach me to leave all things in your hands,
    certain that what you have promised
    you will deliver.
Amen.

Ezekiel 11:17a, 19-20

A different heart and a new spirit

These are the words of the Lord God: I will give them a different heart and put a new spirit into them; I will take the heart of stone out of their bodies and give them a heart of flesh. Then they will conform to my statutes and keep my laws. They will become my people and I will become their God.

Reflection

In December 1967, Dr Christiaan Barnard performed the first human heart transplant at Groote Schuur Hospital in South Africa. It was an operation that stunned and enthralled the world, for few had believed it could ever be achieved. In those early days, life-expectancy for the patient was relatively short; today, this miracle of modern science means a new beginning and a fresh chapter in life for innumerable people.

The words of Ezekiel are figurative rather than literal, yet the transplant they speak of is no less dramatic – if anything, it is more so – for what the prophet is talking about is people being changed not physically but spiritually. Can that really happen? Not according to worldly wisdom. 'A leopard cannot change its spots,' we say; 'Once a thief always a thief.' It's hard as life goes by not to share such a cynical view of the human psyche.

The people of Ezekiel's day felt much the same, greeting his words with scepticism if not outright scorn. Quite simply, they'd heard it all before. Experience had taught them that they would go on making the same mistakes in the future as they had in the past. Ezekiel, though, believed differently, confident that God had the power to change people deep within. His words, of course, were to find fulfilment in the coming of Jesus and the gift of the Holy Spirit. Through Christ, the work of renewal has begun; work that will continue until the day we are united with him in the kingdom of God. Never lose sight of that promise. Never forget what God has done or what he shall yet do.

Prayer

Gracious God,
     have mercy on me,
     pardon my weakness
     and renew me through your Holy Spirit.
Put a new heart and a right spirit within me.
Take what I can never change,
     and, by your grace, make me new.
Amen.

Daniel 3:13-14, 16-18
The fiery furnace

Then in a blinding rage, Nebuchadnezzar ordered Shadrach, Meshach and Abednego to be brought in; so they were hauled before the king. Nebuchadnezzar said to them, 'Is it true, Shadrach, Meshach and Abednego, that you do not serve my gods or worship the golden statue I have had erected?' Shadrach, Meshach and Abednego answered the king, 'O Nebuchadnezzar, we have no need to answer to you concerning this matter. If any god is able to deliver us from the fiery furnace, then it is *our* God, and he will deliver us from your hand, O king. But if not, let us tell you this, O king, we will not serve your gods and will not worship the golden image that you have set up.'

Reflection

The story of Shadrach, Meshach and Abednego is one of the great biblical classics, an unforgettable tale of courage and the triumph of good over evil that has captured the hearts of countless generations. Yet, as with all classics, there is a danger that familiarity may inure us to the wonder of the message. We read the story, knowing the outcome of events – for Shadrach, Meshach and Abednego there was no such luxury. They staked all in the faith that God would deliver them, risking death itself rather than compromise their convictions.

Have we that same faith in God's power? Do we have even a fraction of the astonishing trust these three men displayed? They knew that whatever trials they might face and whatever conspired against God's purpose, nothing finally could thwart him. Remember that next time you feel up against it, the demands of life too great and your resources to meet them too small. Remember that we too can say with confidence, 'If any god is able to deliver us, then it is *our* God.'

Prayer

God of past, present and future,
    I thank you that whatever I may face,
    whatever dangers may threaten me,
    you are able to deliver me from evil.
In life and in death you are by my side,
    nothing able to separate me
    from the wonder of your love.
Help me, then, to put my hand in yours
    and to walk with you wherever you may lead,
    knowing that you will walk by my side,
    this day and always.
Amen.

Hosea 11:1, 3-4, 8-9
A love that will not let me go

When Israel was a child, I loved him, calling my son out of Egypt. I was the one who taught my people Ephraim to walk, who cradled them in my arms; but they did not know that I was the one who nurtured them. I restrained them with love and led them with cords of kindness. Like doting parents lifting their offspring to their cheek, I knelt down to feed them. How can I let you go, Ephraim, and Israel, how can I relinquish you? How can I make you like Admah or treat you like Zeboiim? My heart flinches within me; my devotion burns tenderly within me. I will not give vent to my fury; I will not again destroy Ephraim; for I am God, not human, the Holy One among you, and I will not come in anger.

Reflection

We talk a lot about the love of God but I wonder how many of us have even begun to grasp it. Most people, I suspect, think of God in terms of judgement as much as grace; as a somewhat stern and forbidding father ready to reach out and punish us the moment we step out of line.

Certainly there are times when discipline is necessary but, as the wonderful words of Hosea make clear, this is never something God takes pleasure in administering. Taking his own broken marriage as a model, the prophet paints a graphic and moving picture of the anguish God feels at the repeated rejection and betrayal of his people. Here is an unforgettable glimpse of a love that finally will not let us go, however much we may throw against it. Few passages can more beautifully portray the true nature of the God we serve.

Prayer

Merciful God,
   encircle me,
   nurture me,
   guide and protect me,
   for I am weak and foolish,
   in so many ways still a child.
In your great love,
   stay close
   and watch over me always,
   through Jesus Christ my Lord.
Amen.

Amos 5:18-24

An outer veneer

You who yearn for the day of the Lord are fools, for what will that day actually mean to you? It will be darkness, not light; as though you have fled from a lion only to be met by a bear; or taken refuge in a house only to be bitten by a snake as you rest a hand against the wall. That is what the day of the Lord will be like: unrelieved darkness, night with no prospect of dawn. I loathe and reject your festivals, and take no pleasure in your sacred rituals. Bring me your animal sacrifices and cereal offerings if you must – I will not accept them; I want nothing to do with the atoning sacrifices of your fatted animals. Take away from me the clamour of your songs; I will not listen to the tune of your harps. Instead, let justice cascade down like a mighty river, and righteousness like an inexhaustible stream.

Reflection

One of the gifts I most admire in people is the ability to speak frankly, even when the truth may hurt. There are right and wrong ways of doing this, of course, honesty always needing to be coupled with sensitivity, but the person we can depend on for a candid answer, come what may, is a priceless treasure indeed. Amos was such a one. The message God gave him to speak was bound to be unpopular, yet he knew that the words needed saying and he did not flinch from his call to be the bearer. I doubt many enjoyed what they heard, but those who were willing to listen would have gained a new understanding of what it means to know and love God.

What of us? Perhaps I'm wrong, but I suspect the prophet's words are as much for you and me today as for those who initially heard them. Our practice of religion may be exemplary yet mask a hollow interior. The faith we profess may sound wonderful but be utterly denied by the lives we lead. Our relationship with God can all too easily be confined to Sunday worship, failing to spill over into daily life. True commitment to God involves an equal commitment to others, and to expressing his love for all through word *and* deed, working together to promote his kingdom and further his will. To take the message of Amos seriously may prove a salutary experience. Have we the courage to face it?

Prayer

Lord,
    I'm happy to go to church week by week,
    less sure about reaching out to the world;
    I've no problem offering you worship
    but find it so hard living to your glory.
Forgive me for taking the easy option,
    the way of outward show rather than inner commitment.
Forgive me for divorcing faith from daily life.
Move within me now,
    so that the words of my lips
    may show themselves in the thoughts of my heart
    and the sincerity of my service.
Amen.